FUNdamental Experiments

Air

by Ellen Lawrence

Consultants:

Suzy Gazlay, MA
Recipient, Presidential Award for Excellence in Science Teaching

Kimberly Brenneman, PhD
National Institute for Early Education Research, Rutgers University, New Brunswick, New Jersey

BEARPORT PUBLISHING

Minneapolis, Minnesota

Credits

Cover, © italianestro/Shutterstock and © Roblan/Shutterstock; 2–3, © CoraMax/Shutterstock and © Lukiyanova Natalia/frenta/Shutterstock; 4L, © Brian A. Jackson/Shutterstock; 4R, © S. Curtis/Shutterstock; 5T, © wavebreakmedia/Shutterstock; 5BL, © CoraMax/Shutterstock; 5BR, © Kamira/Shutterstock and © ffoto29/Shutterstock; 6–7, © CoraMax/Shutterstock, © Neil Overy/Shutterstock, and © SmileStudio/Shutterstock; 8–9, © CoraMax/Shutterstock and © Brian A. Jackson/Shutterstock; 10–11, © CoraMax/Shutterstock and © Amero/Shutterstock; 12–13, © CoraMax/Shutterstock, © Neil Overy/Shutterstock, and © rprongjai/Shutterstock; 14–15, © CoraMax/Shutterstock, © Mikhail Mishchenko/Shutterstock, © KPG_Payless/Shutterstock, and © Mega Pixel/Shutterstock; 16–17, © CoraMax/Shutterstock, © rook76/Shutterstock, and © Alexey V Smirnov/Shutterstock; 18–19, © CoraMax/Shutterstock, © artzenter/Shutterstock, © a_v_d/Shutterstock, and © Imageman/Shutterstock; 20–21, © CoraMax/Shutterstock, © jocic/Shutterstock, © SmileStudio/Shutterstock, © rprongjai/Shutterstock, © rook76/Shutterstock, and © Alexey V Smirnov/Shutterstock; 22TL, © Zorandim/Shutterstock; 22TR, © ABBYDOG/Shutterstock; 22BL, © Image Point Fr/Shutterstock; 22BR, © Gary James Calder/Shutterstock; 23, © CoraMax/Shutterstock, © Vasilyev/Shutterstock, © Jaimie Duplass/Shutterstock, and © Sashkin/Shutterstock.

Publisher: Kenn Goin
Editor: Jessica Rudolph
Creative Director: Spencer Brinker
Design: Emma Randall
Photo Researcher: Ruby Tuesday Books Ltd.

Library of Congress Cataloging-in-Publication Data

Lawrence, Ellen, 1967– author.
Air / by Ellen Lawrence.
pages cm. — (FUN-damental experiments)
Includes bibliographical references and index.
ISBN 978-1-62724-539-5 (library binding) — ISBN 1-62724-539-1 (library binding) — ISBN 978-1-64280-780-6 (pbk.)
1. Air—Juvenile literature. 2. Air—Experiments—Juvenile literature. I. Title. II. Series: Lawrence, Ellen, 1967– FUNdamental experiments.
QC161.2.L39 2015
533.6—dc23
2014043306

For more information, write to Bearport Publishing, 5357 Penn Avenue South, Minneapolis MN 55419.
Printed in the United States of America.

Contents

Let's Investigate Air

Air is all around you, and you breathe it in day and night. You usually can't see air, but you can often feel or see it in action—for example, when windy weather blows your hair around. What exactly is air, though? It is a substance made up of tiny, invisible **molecules** of **gases** that people, plants, and animals need to survive. Now it's time to study air like a scientist. Inside this book are lots of fun experiments and cool facts about air. So grab a notebook, and let's investigate!

Check It Out!

You usually can't see air, but you can prove it's around you. Let's check it out!

1. Blow on a pinwheel and see how it spins.

▶ **What is making the pinwheel move?**

2. Wave a book up and down or from side to side in front of your face, like a fan. You will feel a breeze.

▶ **What do you think is happening?**

3. Blow into a balloon and watch as it grows bigger.

▶ **What makes the balloon swell up?**

(The answers are on page 24.)

Does air have weight?

If you hold out your hands and make them into a bowl shape, they will be filled with air. You can't see the air or feel that it's there, though. So does air have weight? Let's investigate!

You will need:

- Three pieces of string each measuring 18 inches (46 cm) long
- A ruler
- An adult helper
- Two balloons
- A pin
- A notebook and pencil

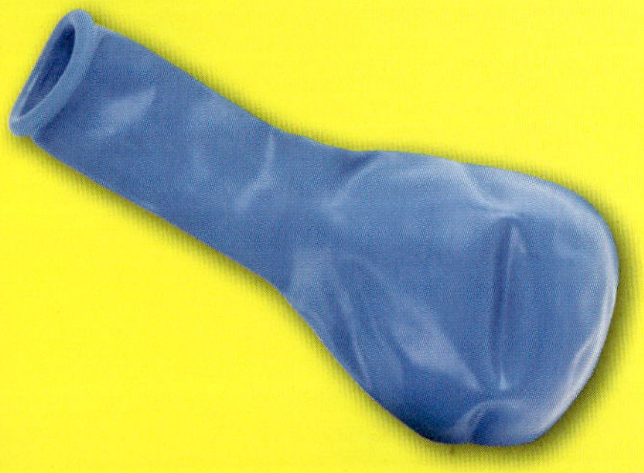

1. Tie one piece of string around the center of a ruler.

2. Ask an adult helper to blow up a balloon and tie the end with a knot. Have the adult blow up the second balloon so it's the same size as the first, and knot the end.

3. Tie a piece of string around the knot of each balloon. Then tie the balloons' strings to the ruler 1 inch (2.5 cm) from the ends.

4 Hold the string in the center of the ruler and let the balloons hang down. The ruler will be **level** because the two balloons weigh the same.

- **What do you think will happen to the ruler if you pop one of the balloons?**

Write your **predictions** in your notebook.

In your notebook, record everything you observed.

- **What happened to the ruler?**
- **Do you think the balloons still weigh the same?**
- **Do you think air has weight? Why or why not?**

5 Ask your adult helper to pop one balloon with a pin.

(To learn more about this investigation and find the answers to the questions, see pages 20-21.)

Does air push against things?

If you sit in a room where the air is still, you can't feel the air around you. The air is definitely there, though, and it's exerting a **force**, or pushing, on everything in the room—including you! This force is called **air pressure**. If you can't feel the air pressure around you, though, how can you be sure it's really there? Let's investigate!

You will need:

- An empty 1 liter (34 oz) plastic bottle
- Water
- A bowl
- A long straw
- Modeling clay
- A notebook and pencil

1. Fill a bottle three-quarters full with water. Place the bottle in the bowl.

2. Put a straw into the bottle so one end is in the water. Make sure there is about 3 inches (7.6 cm) of the straw sticking out of the opening of the bottle.

3. Wrap the modeling clay around the bottle's opening and the straw. Seal the opening so no air can get in or out.

▶ **What do you think will happen if you blow into the straw?**

Write your prediction in your notebook.

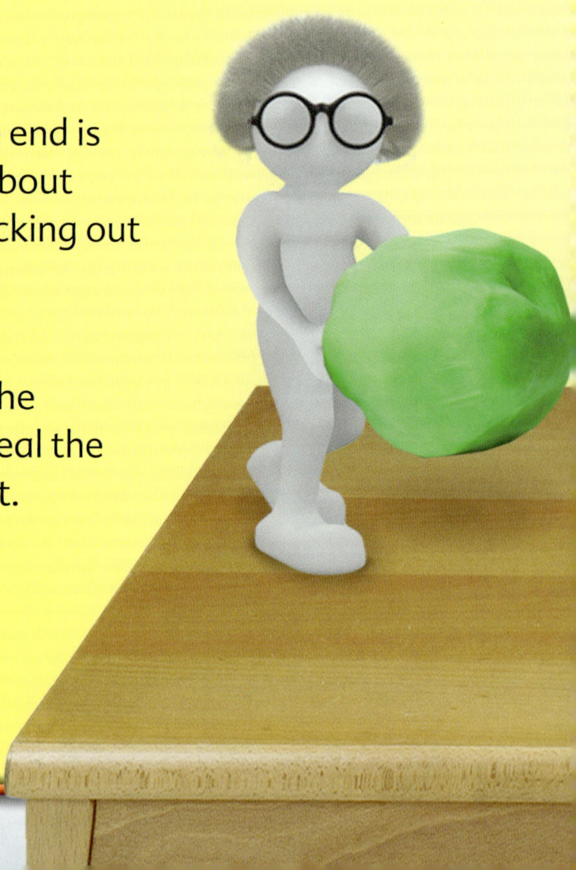

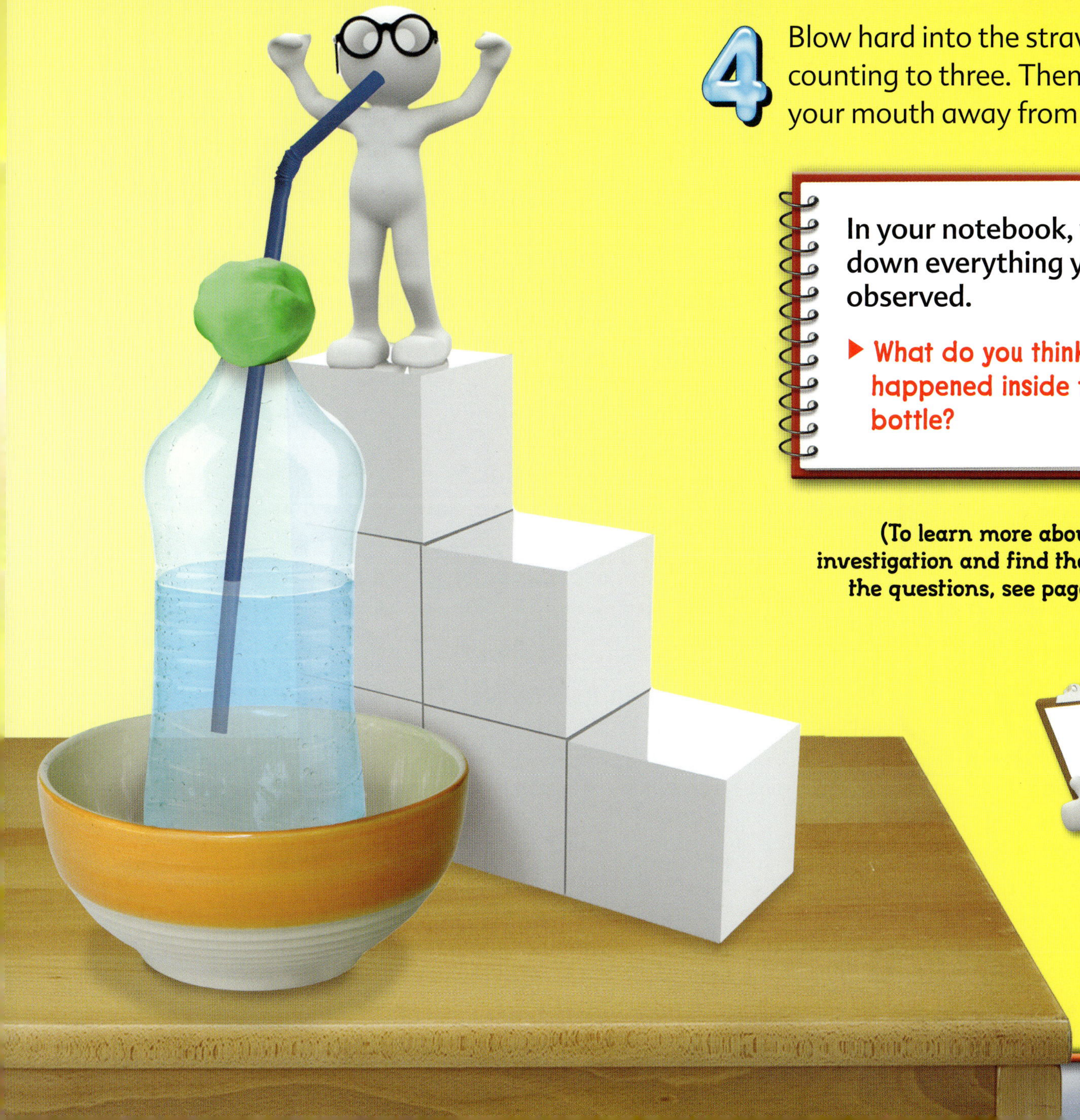

4 Blow hard into the straw while counting to three. Then quickly take your mouth away from the straw.

In your notebook, write down everything you observed.

- ▶ **What do you think happened inside the bottle?**

(To learn more about this investigation and find the answers to the questions, see pages 20–21.)

Can air slow down a falling object?

When you drop an object, it falls to the ground because of a force called **gravity**. This force pulls all things—even you—toward the ground. You've discovered, though, that air can act as a force, too. So can air affect the pull of gravity?

You will need:

- Two sheets of paper that are identical, and therefore weigh the same
- A notebook and pencil

1. Hold a sheet of paper so it is flat, like a tabletop.

   ▶ **What do you think will happen if you drop the paper?**

2. Now drop the paper and observe what happens.

3 Take the second sheet of paper and crumple it up into a tight ball.

- **If you drop both pieces of paper at the same time, what do you think will happen?**

Write your prediction in your notebook.

4 Drop both pieces of paper at exactly the same time and observe what happens.

In your notebook, write down what happened.

- **Did your prediction match the results of the experiment?**
- **How do you think the air under the paper affected what happened?**

(To learn more about this investigation and find the answers to the questions, see pages 20–21.)

Does hot air act differently from cold air?

Depending on the weather, the air outside can feel cold or hot. Air feels different to us when its **temperature** changes. Do the molecules in air act differently, though, depending on if they are hot or cold? Let's find out!

1. Stretch a balloon over the neck of an empty bottle. Then stand the bottle in a bowl of hot water. Hold the bottle firmly to stop it from floating in the water.

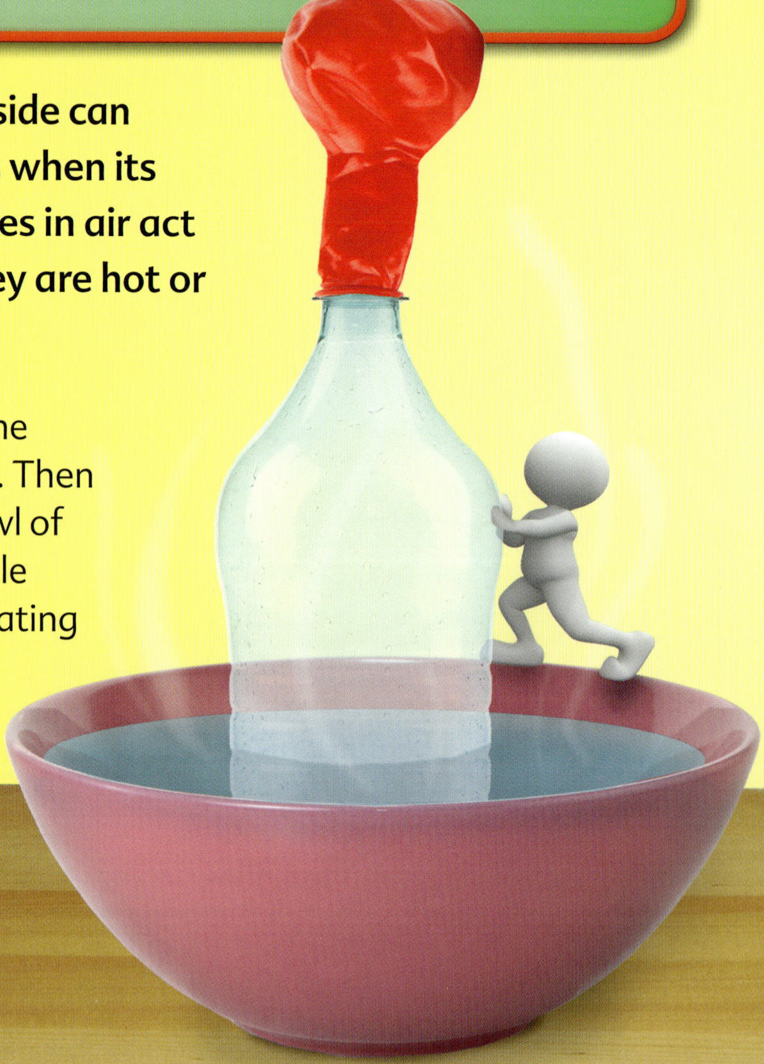

You will need:

- A balloon
- An empty 1 liter (34 oz) plastic bottle
- A bowl half filled with hot water from the tap
- A bowl half filled with water and ice cubes
- A notebook and pencil

2 Observe everything that takes place.

- **What happens to the balloon?**
- **What do you think the air inside the bottle is doing?**

3 Place the bottle in the bowl of ice water.

- **What happened to the balloon?**

In your notebook, write down everything you observed.

- **What do you think happened to the air in the bottle when it was heated by the hot water?**
- **What happened to the air in the bottle when it was cooled by the ice water?**

(To learn more about this investigation and find the answers to the questions, see pages 20–21.)

What's in air?

You know that air is made up of molecules of gases. What else is in air, though? In this next experiment, you will make a catching **device** so you can closely examine the tiny objects floating in air.

You will need:

- A notebook and pencil
- A hole punch
- A waterproof, disposable plate
- A piece of string about 24 inches (61 cm) long
- Petroleum jelly
- A magnifying glass

1 Look outside.

- Do you see anything floating in the air?
- What kinds of things do you think could be floating in the air that you don't see?

Write your observations and ideas in your notebook.

2 Make a catching device. Use a hole punch to make a hole in the edge of a plate. Tie a string to the plate through the hole. Then tie the ends of the string together to make a loop.

3 Use your hand to smear a layer of petroleum jelly on one side of the plate.

4 Hang your catching device outside. For example, you can hang it from a tree branch.

5 After two days, bring the device inside and examine it closely.

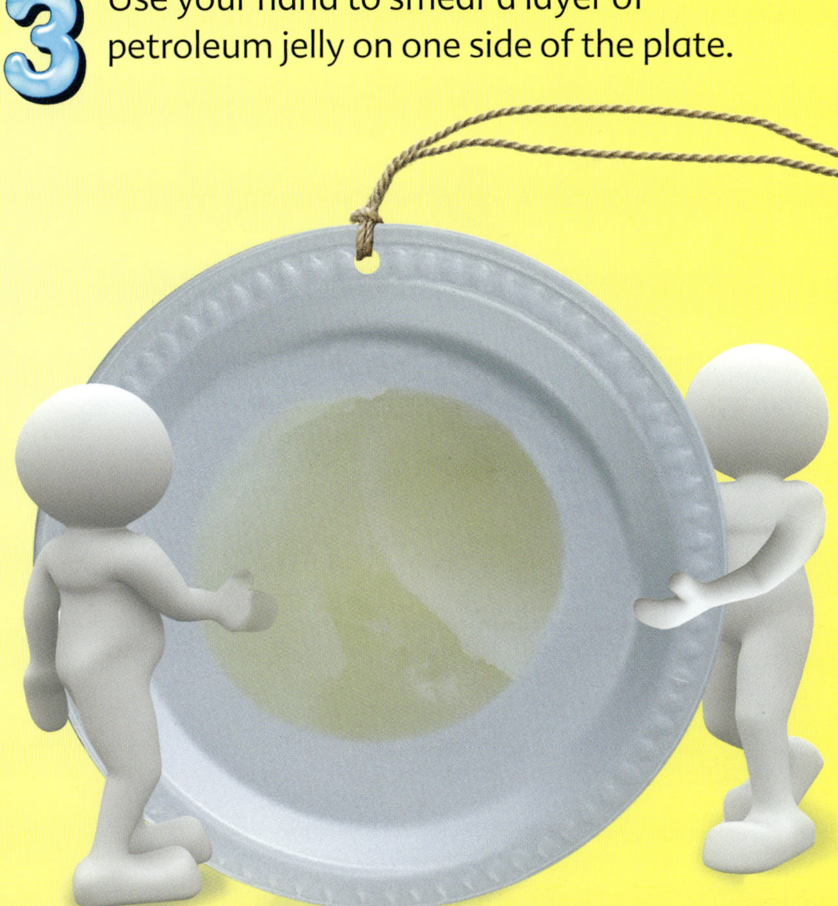

In your notebook, write down everything you see on your catching device.

- **What can you see using only your eyes?**
- **What do you see if you look at it using a magnifying glass?**

(To learn more about this investigation and find the answers to the questions, see pages 20–21.)

Is there water in air?

You know that air is made up of gases and tiny solid particles. Now let's find out if air also contains liquids. Do you think it's possible that there is water in the air inside your home or classroom? Let's investigate!

1 Fill a glass with ice and stand the glass in a bowl.

You will need:

- Two glasses
- Ice cubes
- Two bowls
- A notebook and pencil

2 Stand the second glass in another bowl. This glass will be empty.

3 Let the glasses stand for one hour.

After one hour, the glass with the ice cubes will be wet on the outside. The bowl that contains this glass may even have water in it. The other glass and bowl will be dry.

- It's not possible for the water on the outside of the first glass to have come from inside the glass, so where do you think it came from?
- Do you think the air inside your home or classroom contains water? Why do you think so?

(To learn more about this investigation and find the answers to the questions, see pages 20–21.)

Can smells travel through air?

The molecules of gases that make up air don't have a smell. When we sniff the air, however, we can often notice lots of different **odors**, or smells. So what is a smell? A smell is made of tiny molecules that are much too small to see. How do smells reach our noses, though? Let's investigate!

You will need:

- A helper
- Three cotton balls
- Five small containers with lids
- Lemon juice
- Perfume
- Vinegar
- A mashed banana
- Mashed garlic
- A scarf for a blindfold
- A notebook and pencil

1 Ask your helper to leave the room. Then place all your supplies on a table.

2 Soak a cotton ball in lemon juice and then put it in a container and close the lid. Repeat with a cotton ball soaked in perfume and one in vinegar. Put the mashed banana in a container and close the lid. Repeat with the mashed garlic.

3 Ask your helper to come into the room and stand about 3 feet (0.9 m) from the table. The helper should cover his or her eyes with a scarf.

4 Open the container that holds the lemon juice. Wave the container in the air. Ask your helper to tell you when he or she smells something. Ask the helper to guess what the smell is.

5 Repeat with the other four containers.

In your notebook, write down everything that happens.

- Did your helper notice each of the smells? Did he or she guess them correctly?
- How do you think the five odors in the containers were able to reach your helper's nose?

(To learn more about this investigation and find the answers to the questions, see pages 20–21.)

Discovery Time

Investigating the world using science is fun! Now, let's check out all the things we discovered about air.

Pages 6–7

Does air have weight?

When you popped one balloon, the other balloon pulled one end of the ruler down, so the ruler was no longer level. That's because the balloon that still has air in it is heavier than the popped, or empty, balloon. The air inside the balloon makes it heavier. This shows that air has weight.

Pages 8–9

Does air push against things?

Three-quarters of the bottle was filled with water. The other quarter was filled with air. When you blew into the straw, you increased the amount of air—and therefore air pressure—in the bottle. The air pushed down on the water. This forced the water to shoot up the straw like a fountain! The air pressure was so great it actually made the water move.

Pages 10–11

Can air slow down a falling object?

It might seem that because the two pieces of paper weigh the same, they would fall to the ground at exactly the same time. However, the ball of paper hits the ground first. Why? Gravity pulls both pieces of paper down to the ground. At the same time, air is pushing up against the pieces of paper as they fall. The ball of paper is smaller in size than the flat sheet of paper. This means there is less air pushing up against it, so the crumpled paper falls faster. The flat sheet of paper is bigger in size, so there is more air pushing up against it. This makes the sheet of paper fall more slowly.

Pages 12–13

Does hot air act differently from cold air?

Air molecules are always moving around. When air molecules are heated, they move faster. When they are cooled, they slow down. As the air molecules inside the bottle and balloon warmed up, they began to move around faster and faster, bouncing off the insides of the bottle and balloon. This fast movement made the air expand, or take up more room, causing the balloon to swell up. Once the bottle was placed in the ice water, the air molecules slowed down. This caused the air to contract, or take up less room, and the balloon became smaller again.

Pages 14–15

What's in air?

Your catching device might have caught tiny bits of dust or dirt. These solid particles may have come from vehicle exhausts and construction sites. Soot in the smoke from fires also floats in the air, as do tiny bits of sand and soil and powdery dust from flowers and trees, called pollen. You may also have caught small leaves, seeds, and insects. It's not always possible to see tiny solid particles in the air, but they are there!

Pages 16–17

Is there water in the air?

You can't see it, but air contains water. Even the air inside buildings has water, although the water isn't liquid like rain. Instead, it is in the form of a gas called water vapor. When water vapor gets cold enough, it changes into liquid water. In your experiment, water vapor in the air touched the cold glass that was filled with ice cubes. The vapor became cold and turned into liquid water. The empty glass was not cold. Therefore, when water vapor in the air touched this glass, it did not turn into a liquid.

Pages 18–19

Can smells travel through air?

When you opened the containers, tiny molecules of smelly gases floated into the air. They floated among the other gas molecules, water vapor, and solid particles until they reached your helper's nose. Then they floated up his or her nose and were smelled by your helper.

Air in Your World

Air doesn't do exciting things only during scientific experiments. Check out the ways that you can see air in action in the world around you!

1. A skydiver jumps from a plane and floats to the ground using a parachute.

▶ **How does a parachute help the skydiver fall slowly?**

2. Sometimes, a person accidentally burns toast in the kitchen.

▶ **Why can you smell the burned toast throughout your home?**

3. Sometimes, the air makes a person sneeze, cough, or have trouble breathing.

▶ **Why do you think this happens?**

4. On a cold winter morning, water sometimes appears on the inside of the windows in your home.

▶ **Where did the water come from?**

Answers:

1. A parachute is very large. There is a lot of air beneath the parachute pushing on it. The air pushing against the parachute makes the skydiver fall slowly. **2.** Tiny, smelly molecules of gases from the burned toast float through the air, spreading throughout your home, so you notice the burned smell from far away. **3.** Small, solid particles of dirt in the air can make people sneeze, cough, and have trouble breathing. Pollen from plants, smoke from fires, and gases from vehicle exhaust can make people ill, too. **4.** Water vapor in the air inside your home touched the cold window and changed into liquid water.

Science Words

air pressure (AIR PRESH-ur) the force that is created by air pushing on everything

device (di-VYESS) a piece of equipment that does a particular job

force (FORSS) something that causes movement, such as a pull or a push

gases (GASS-iz) matter that floats in air and is neither liquid nor solid; many gases, such as water vapor, are invisible

gravity (GRAV-uh-tee) the force that pulls things toward Earth and keeps them from drifting into space

level (LEV-uhl) having a flat, even surface; horizontal

molecules (MOL-uh-kyoolz) tiny parts of something that are too small to see; for example, water is made up of molecules

odors (OH-durz) another word for *smells*

predictions (pri-DIK-shuhnz) guesses that things will happen in a certain way; they are often based on facts a person knows or things a person has observed

temperature (TEM-pur-uh-chur) a measurement of how hot or cold something is

Index

Read More

Cooper, Sharon Katz. *Using Air (Exploring Earth's Resources).* Chicago: Heinemann (2007).

Green, Jen. *The Air We Breathe (Our Earth).* New York: PowerKids Press (2008).

Lawrence, Ellen. *Dirty Air (Green World, Clean World).* New York: Bearport (2014).

Learn More Online

To learn more about air, visit
www.bearportpublishing.com/FundamentalExperiments

About the Author

Ellen Lawrence lives in the United Kingdom. Her favorite books to write are those about nature and animals. In fact, the first book Ellen bought for herself, when she was six years old, was the story of a gorilla named Patty Cake that was born in New York's Central Park Zoo.

Answers for Page 5

1. You are creating moving air by blowing. This air moves the pinwheel.
2. The movement of the book is making the air move. You feel this moving air as a breeze.
3. You are blowing air into the balloon. This causes the balloon to stretch and expand.